T0167138

DALE'S WAR

A Soldier in Patton's Third Army

ROGER W. HUBLEY

Order this book online at www.trafford.com
or email orders@trafford.com

Most Trafford titles are also available at major online book retailers.

Printed in the United States of America.

ISBN: 978-1-4907-0791-4 (sc)
ISBN: 978-1-4907-0793-8 (hc)
ISBN: 978-1-4907-0792-1 (e)

Library of Congress Control Number: 2013914031

Trafford rev. 08/01/2013

www.trafford.com

North America & international
toll-free: 1 888 232 4444 (USA & Canada)
fax: 812 355 4082

Front cover pictures:

Map
Third Army Dispositions evening 5 September 1944 (Map VI)
(Map credit—Hugh Cole, The Lorraine Campaign)

Seventh Armored Division Insignia
The yellow, blue, and red are the colors of the branches from which armored units were formed—Cavalry, US Regiment of Dragoons, and the Tank Service.
(Photo credit—The Institute of Heraldry, The United States Army)

Gray Ghost
The *Queen Mary* was painted gray during her wartime service.
(Photo credit—Australian War Memorial)

DEDICATION

I never met a man I didn't like.
—Will Rogers

To the service and memory of
Rankin Dale Hubley

Those who knew Dale will understand completely
why the above quotation is used.

CONTENTS

ACKNOWLEDGMENTS

I AM GRATEFUL TO MY wife, Melody, whose continued encouragement to write Dad's stories kept this project on track. Thanks also to my daughters, Susan Kneidl, Jill Chupka, and Amy Stover, for always being interested in their grandfather's World War II stories. It was always helpful to have my wife, daughters, and their three husbands willing to read the manuscript and offer suggestions and improvements to my writings.

There were many friends who helped with their encouragement and by reading and critiquing the manuscript. Two who made me feel that I really should share my father's stories were Bonnie and Ken Rupe. Thank you!

I want to thank other friends and family who helped by reading the manuscript or just listening to the stories and providing encouragement to get Dad's stories published. This list includes Jeff and Jan Simons, Art and Donna McBeath, Dave and Carol Lenert, and Denny and Carol Kramer.

I want to also thank Tom and Karen Hartman for traveling with my wife and me in 2012 as we followed the first half of Dad's route through France. The narrow roads, getting lost, being stuck in roundabouts, and eating French pastries—a memorable trip!

Thanks also to the Seventh Armored Division Association. Their history books, volume 1 and volume 2, provide a wealth of information. Also, thanks to the Seventh Armored Division Association website that provided the links to After Action Reports, Morning Reports, Unit Histories, and other valuable information.

And finally, a special thanks to the citizens of Sillegny, France. It was an honor to visit your lovely town and meet so many friendly people. Thank you, Jean-Marc Grunfelder for your friendship, your time, and your caring. Thank you, Jean-Marc Tabard, for keeping the history of the Seventh Armored Division's action at Sillegny alive, and thank you, Mayor Francois Lespagnol, for your gifts and writing my father's story in the local paper. It was an emotional visit for my wife and me. Thank you for remembering.

INTRODUCTION

M Y FATHER, RANKIN DALE Hubley, served in Patton's Third Army during World War II. His first name was Rankin, but he always went by his middle name, Dale. I grew up listening to his war stories as he was always willing to share his experiences in the war, unlike many veterans. He was a good storyteller, and my brother and I enjoyed his stories as did anyone else who would ask him about the war. As I got older, Dad would share more of his stories with me and go into greater detail. Some had gruesome details; some were funny, and a few he asked me never to tell anyone else—and I never have or will. In 1991, I decided to preserve his stories. I started by taking sheets of typing paper, and on the top of a page, I would write a short summary of a story that I remembered him telling me—one story per page. I gave this stack of pages to Dad, and I asked him to finish "the rest of the story," as Paul Harvey would say—one of his favorite radio programs. After about two years, he had completed, in his own handwriting, the project. In addition to his written memories, I taped some of his thoughts. I took Dad to see the Patton Museum at Fort Knox, Kentucky, and brought along a tape recorder with me in the car. As we drove down and back, he told stories, and I recorded them. I loved seeing the Patton Museum through his eyes and listening to what he would say about the different exhibits. I then transcribed all this information into a booklet of Dale's World War II stories. Many friends and family have read and enjoyed these memories. Dad was ninety-one years old when he died in 1997.

I had always wanted to take a trip to France and follow the route he took during the war. I started doing research on the Third Army, the XX Corps, the Seventh Armored Division, and the Thirty-eighth Armored Infantry Battalion. I set up a timeline based on information from his diary, After Action Reports of the various units, Morning Reports of the units, GI stories, and from the Seventh Armored Division Association history books, volumes 1 and 2. Dad had many mementoes from the war, but the one I prize the most is his boarding pass from the *Queen Mary*. He had the boarding pass with him when he boarded the *Queen* on June 6, 1944, in New York and carried the card in his helmet through France. As his outfit would pass through towns in France, he would write down the name of the town and the date on the card. I have that card and used it to map his route through France with the Seventh Armored Division. My wife and I followed the first half of his route in 2012 and went back to finish tracing his route in 2013. It was very moving to see the land and towns that he went through and to stand in some of the very places where he fought.

It is not the intent of this book to write a history of the Seventh Armored Division; other books cover that topic. Rather, it is to chronicle the life of my father—who he was and his service in World War II. Where I have included historical references, it is to provide a background to his story and what he was going through. All the stories are from either my father's writings or his tape-recorded recollections. Some of the stories I have paraphrased, but all the stories in quotations are written directly as told by my father, the only corrections made for spelling errors.

Everyone said I should write a book using my father's stories from World War II. So I did.

Rankin Dale Hubley

Third Army
> Gen. George S. Patton

XX Corps
> Maj. Gen. Walton H. Walker

Seventh Armored Division
> Maj. Gen. Lindsay M. Silvester

Thirty-Eighth Armored Infantry Battalion
> Lt. Col. Edwin L. Keeler (until 11 Sept. '44)

Company A
> Capt. Dan Jennings

Third Rifle Platoon
> 2nd Lt. Walter H. G. Weissenberger

These town names were transcribed from the card carried in Dale's helmet as he moved through France with the Seventh Armored Division.

August 13, 1944
    Saint-Lo
    Gavray
    La Haye-Pesnel
    Avranches
    Ducey
    Louvigne-du-Desert

August 14
    Ernee
    Change
    Laval
    Evron
    Rouesse-Vasse
    Peze-le-Robert
    Beaumont-sur-Sarthe
    La Ferte-Bernard

August 15
    Nogent-le-Rotrou
    Glatigny
    La Closure

August 16
    Courville-sur-Eure (action in town)
    Leves
    Jouy

August 17 and 18 fought in Chartres

August 19
    Chateauneuf-en-Thymerais
    Dreux (overnight)

August 20
    Marolles

August 22
    Etrechy
    Boissy-le-Cutte
    Monceau
    Orgenoy
    Melun

August 23, 24, 25
    Melun

August 26
    Ponthierry
    Fontainebleau

August 27
    Hericy
    Le Chatelet-en-Brie
    Nangis (start of drive)

August 28
    La Forestiere
    Barbonne-Fayel
    Mareuil-en-Brie

August 29
    Moussy
    Pierry
    Epernay
    Damery
    [Thuisey]

August 30
    Tagnon
    Avancon

August 31
    Verdun (and around)

August 21
    Maintenon   September 6
    Hanches   Haudiomont
    Bleury
    Albis
    Sainte-Mesme
    Dourdan

PROLOGUE

B ECAUSE OF BEING POPULARIZED in books, movies, and/or on television, many people know about or have heard of the following: Operation Overlord, D-Day, Operation Cobra, the Falaise Pocket, Patton's dash across France, Operation Market Garden, the Remagen Bridge, Patton's December move north to Bastogne, and the Battle of the Bulge.

Unfortunately, few people know about the Lorraine Campaign as it has come to be referred to historically. Patton's Third Army had the Germans retreating, and by September 1, 1944, it seemed that he would be able to push into Germany and, some thought, end the war by Christmas. Unfortunately, on September 1, the Third Army's gas supply was halted. The inability of Patton to continue his advance allowed the Germans to reinforce a line roughly on the east side of the Moselle River from north of Metz to south of Nancy.[1] These two towns were the thrust of the Third Army's sector. The Seventh Army landed south of Cannes in Southern France on August 15, 1944. Operation Dragoon had the Seventh Army moving north through France on the Third Army's right flank.[2] The First Army was moving toward the east on the left flank north of Patton's sector.[3]

The fighting during the Lorraine Campaign lasted from the September 1, 1944 until December 19, 1944. During this three-month period, the Third Army moved only from the Moselle River to the Saar River. This is a distance of about thirty miles to the east of Metz. It was during this fighting near Metz that the war, for my father, became painfully real.

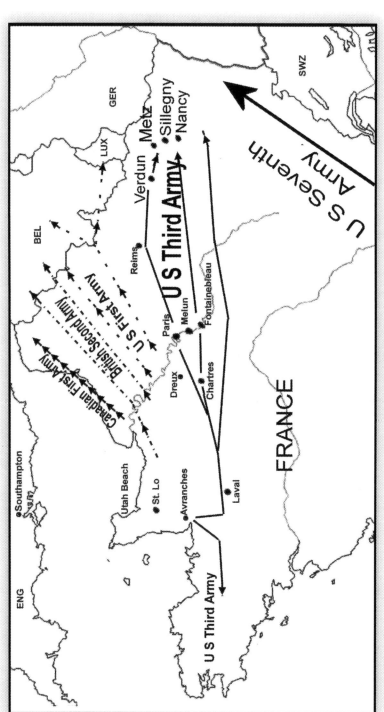

Fig. 1. Hubley map

First, Third, and Seventh Army movement through France

CHAPTER 1

———◆•◆•◆———

Drafted

1906-1942
Dayton to Cincinnati

D ALE WAS BORN IN Dayton, Ohio, in 1906. The family lived at 409 E. Lowes Street, not far from the Wright Brothers bicycle shop. Today, the house is used as housing for the University of Dayton. He had a younger brother, Myron, and an older sister, Annamae. Dale's father, Walter D. Hubley, was a railroad postal clerk. He worked for the United States Postal Service sorting mail in the mail car as the train traveled from town to town.

In 1912, Walter was transferred, and the family moved from Dayton to Hartwell, a suburb of Cincinnati, Ohio. The family lived at 8122 Woodbine Avenue. Dale attended high school at Hartwell and then went to the University of Cincinnati for a short time. His sister, unfortunately, had a nervous breakdown after her senior year in high school, and Dale's life would change. The breakdown was so severe that he left school to work and help the family. Within a few years, Annamae was committed to Longview State Mental Hospital where she would spend the remainder of her life (about seventy years). Annamae died when she was ninety-three years old. For the rest of his life, Dale would faithfully go visit Annamae even though she did not recognize her brother.

Dale met his future wife, Wanda, at a church dinner. Both were attending the Hartwell Methodist Church young adult class. Wanda had graduated from Miami University and was teaching elementary school in Hartwell. He had seen Wanda and wanted to meet her. So at this dinner, Dale switched name tags to sit next to her. Asked why he switched name tags, he would always say, "She was the littlest thing I ever saw, and she didn't have any shoes because she grew up in the hills of Kentucky!" Wanda was small, but she had shoes and grew up in Ohio, not Kentucky. He always liked kidding people by telling them that story.

Dale and Wanda were married in August of 1935.

Fig. 2. Hubley photo

Dale and Wanda wedding photo

Before being married, Dale had worked as a car salesman, then at Sawbrook Steel Castings Co., for a time at Lunken Airport in Cincinnati, and soon after being married, got a job at Procter & Gamble in the Duncan Hines product-testing laboratory. He was able to bring home cakes that they tested in the lab—a great perk. In 1940, his salary at Procter & Gamble was $1,560 per year. Later, he worked in a laboratory at P&G running tests for color, specific gravity, and other specifications in the soap-making factory.

In October of 1942, their first son, Alan, was born. Dale had worked at Procter & Gamble for about eight years and had a good job. The future looked bright for his family.

July 1943-May 1944
Cincinnati to Tyler, Texas

Then, on July 15, 1943, Dale received his induction notice in the mail. He was thirty-seven years old and had been drafted into the army. While many men were drafted during World War II, not many were thirty-seven years old. It came as a great shock when he opened his "Welcome to the Army" letter. But if you asked him about being drafted at his age, he would be very matter-of-fact and say, "They needed cannon fodder." No one ever heard Dale complain or gripe about being older and being drafted. He did his duty, served his country, and eventually came home. After the war, he was never bitter. He would tell people that he was one of the lucky ones because, in his words, "I got to come home." He was truly one of the "greatest generation."

Fig. 3. Hubley photo

Dale in uniform

Fig. 4. Hubley photo

Dale, Wanda, Alan

He was processed into the army at Fort Thomas, Kentucky. To get to Fort Thomas, he boarded a train at Cincinnati Union Terminal. It was here that he saw his father for the last time. Dale's mom said that his father was a war causality dying from a broken heart.

The group that he had been assigned to was being shipped out for basic training, but they were not told where they were going because of security. The draftees boarded a troop train at Fort Thomas, which had all the curtains pulled except for a small three-inch opening at the bottom. They were told that they could open the windows a couple of inches to get some air. After boarding the train, the draftees were then told that they were headed for Texas. At that time, Dale and his wife, Wanda, lived in Hartwell, Ohio, a subdivision of Cincinnati. Even though the shades were pulled, he could tell he was going through Cincinnati. A short time later, the train stopped, and he recognized that the train had stopped at the Reading train station that was near his home in Hartwell. Why the train stopped in Reading, he didn't know, but when the train stopped, children from all around would come to wave at the troops in the train. Dale wrote a note on the inside of a matchbook cover. The note said, "Call Wanda. Tell her I'm on my way to Texas." He wrote the note hoping a child would see it and then, after adding his home phone number, tossed the matchbook out of the train window. He pointed to the matchbook laying on the platform, and a boy picked it up. The boy's mom called Wanda, and that is how she learned that he had been shipped out. During the war, there was much secrecy about troop movements. Dale later wondered if he would have been arrested had he been caught tossing the matchbook out the window!

Fig. 5. US Army photo

Fifty-second Battalion, Company C at Camp Fannin

Dale arrived at Tyler, Texas, in August of 1943. Basic training was at Camp Fannin and lasted about six months. He was assigned to the Eleventh Training Regiment, Fifty-Second Battalion, Company C, First Platoon. Camp Fannin was a US Army Infantry Replacement Training Center and POW Camp. It was opened in 1943 and only operated for four years before closing in 1946. Over two hundred thousand troops trained there with as many as forty thousand at any given time.[4]

After basic training, his battalion was to be sent to North Africa, but at the last minute, he was pulled out of line to wait for glasses to be made for his gas mask. There was much concern that the Germans would use gas in World War II the same as they had used it in World War I. Dale later learned that many of the men in his company became casualties in North Africa. This was one time he was glad he wore glasses. He was at Tyler, Texas, for about three or four more weeks.

Toward the end of January 1944, he was shipped to Fort Benning, Georgia, where he joined the Seventh Armored Division known as the Lucky Seventh. Fort Benning is located on the far west side of Georgia about halfway between Tennessee and Florida. During World War II, the base encompassed 197,159 acres. The military post is known for training infantry at its Infantry School.[5]

May-June 1944
New York to England

From Fort Benning, the division went to Camp Miles Standish. This army camp is located in Taunton, Massachusetts. It functioned as a prisoner-of-war camp and a departure area for about a million US and Allied soldiers.[6] About a week after arriving, the division was to get on a boat to be sent to Europe, but at the last minute, another unit was assigned to the boat. A troop train came in and brought the other GIs to be loaded on the boat. The Seventh Armored Division was put on a second train and taken to Camp Shanks. This was a United States Army installation in and around Orangetown, New York. Situated near the juncture of the Erie Railroad and the Hudson River, it served as a point of embarkation for troops departing overseas during World War II. Dubbed Last Stop USA, the camp housed about fifty thousand troops spread over 2,040 acres and was the largest World War II army embarkation camp, processing 1.3 million service personnel including 75 percent of those participating in the D-Day invasion.[7] A week later, the Seventh Armored Division was brought from Camp Shanks to New York and boarded the *Queen Mary* on June 6, 1944, D-Day morning. Dale said, "What a boat!"

The *Queen Mary* set sail the morning of June 7, 1944, on trip number 36E (the thirty-sixth eastbound crossing) with 11,993 soldiers on board. It took six days to cross the Atlantic—five days, twelve hours, and eighteen minutes to be exact.[8] The room Dale slept in had nine bunk bed cots—three rows of three cots floor to ceiling. So his room slept twenty-seven soldiers! The sleeping arrangements were nine GIs for eight hours at a time. The rest of the time was spent on deck. With so many men on board, only two meals a day were served. The *Queen Mary* had been painted gray for the war and earned the nickname the Gray Ghost.

Fig. 6. US Navy photo

The Gray Ghost

Fig. 7. J. Kent Layton Collection

Troops on deck during crossing

The *Queen Mary* was the largest and fastest troopship during World War II. All troop ships would travel with navy escorts for protection except the *Queen Mary*. She was the only troop ship that did not go in a convoy because she was faster than the escort ships and she could outrun any submarine.[9] She had sonar that could pick up the sound of a sub as far as seven miles away and was never hit by a shell. Dale liked to sit on the back of the boat and watch the wake that the large propellers made as they churned up the water. Sometimes the boat would go sharply to the left or right, other times make a complete circle. The *Queen Mary* carried 765,429 troops during the war and traveled 569,429 miles. Her wartime service lasted from March 1940 through September 1946.[10]

Adolf Hitler offered $250,000 and the Iron Cross to any U-boat captain that could sink the *Queen Mary*. "We knew they [Germans] were trying to get the *Queen* in a pocket," Dale said. "All the way over, she would turn left real sharp, and you could look down the deck at the water, then she would roll over on the other side. In the bunks, we rolled from side to side. What a relief when the *Queen Mary* entered the gates at the Firth of Clyde in Scotland. The *Queen* straightened out and ran straight again."

June-July 1944
England

The *Queen Mary* landed on June 12, 1944, at Gourock, Scotland (near Greenock) in the Firth of Clyde. She anchored in the middle of the River Clyde, a wide body of water. Large boats and ferries took the GIs to the mainland where a troop train was waiting. Because of her size, the *Queen Mary* could only dock at about six places in the world. It went to Scotland because Liverpool and Southampton were patrolled by enemy subs.

Fig. 8. Hubley map

Troop movement from Gourock, Scotland, to Tideworth, England

    The army shipped the men by train to Tideworth Barracks, near Wiltshire, England, north of Southampton. While staying there, the men drew equipment—half tracks, tanks, etc. The Seventh Armored Division was at Tideworth Barracks for about four weeks.

CHAPTER 2

---◆·◆·◆---

Moving through France

August 1-12, 1944
England to France

ON AUGUST 1, 1944, the Third Army was activated with General George Patton as its commanding officer. On August 7 and 8, the Seventh Armored Division moved to Southampton and Portsmouth to begin boarding ships for France. On August 10, the Seventh Armored Division was attached to XX Corp of the Third Army. Units of the Seventh Armored Division began landing at Utah Beach and Omaha Beach between August 10 and 14.[11] Dale's Company A landed on Utah Beach at 0800 August 12, 1944. The crossing was uneventful.[12]

After Dale's company landed on Utah Beach, the GIs were told to drop their duffel bags. Dale never saw his again. He said, "Soon after landing, we were told the Germans and Americans would not use gas. The agreement was a wonderful thing."

August 13, 1944
Utah Beach, France

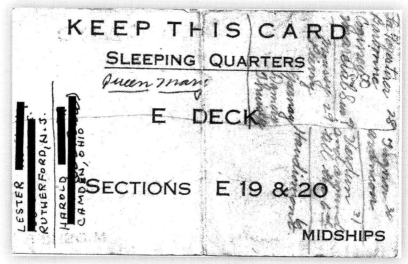

Fig. 9. Hubley photo

Front of boarding card

Fig. 10. Hubley photo

Back of boarding card

Figures 9 and 10 are the front and back of the *Queen Mary* boarding card that Dale used to write down the names of the towns he went through. He kept this card in his helmet as he moved across France. Some of the towns were not spelled correctly because he only had a brief look at the town sign as his half-track was on the move. The half-track was a versatile vehicle that had tanklike tracks on the back and regular wheels on the front. It could carry a rifle squad of twelve men. The half-track Dale rode in had a machine gun mounted toward the front over the cab. During the war, approximately forty-three thousand half-tracks were produced and shipped overseas.[13]

Fig. 11. Cole Land Transportation Museum

Dale's rifle squad rode in half-tracks similar to the one shown

After leaving Utah Beach, Dale's unit went through Saint-Lo and headed south. Saint-Lo had been bombed and shelled so much that a bulldozer was needed to get through all the rubble. Dale did not have his shoes off after landing in France until the end of September when he was wounded. He had problems with his feet for the rest of his life because of this. "Patton's Third Army was on the move, and there was never time to take our boots off," he said.

The Seventh Armored Division was assembling and moving out as quickly as the boats could be unloaded of men and equipment. There was rapid movement through Saint-Lo, Avranches, Ducey, and on to Louvigne-du-Desert.

As the Germans were retreating, they would string piano wire across the road from tree to tree at the right height to cut off the heads of jeep and half-track drivers. The Americans welded an angle iron up from the front bumper to above the driver's head with a sharp hook on top to cut the wire as the vehicle was moving.

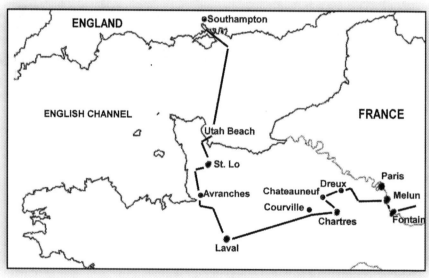

Fig. 12. Hubley map

Map of Dale's movement from Southampton to Melun

August 14, 1944
La Ferte-Bernard

Dale's unit, Company A of the Thirty-Eighth Armored Infantry Battalion (AIB), moved quickly through Ernee, Laval, Beaumont-sur-Sarthe, and on to La Ferte-Bernard. On August 13 and 14, the Thirty-Eighth Armored Infantry Battalion was moving rapidly to catch up with the XX Corps.

August 15, 1944
Nogent-le-Rotrou

Company A of the Thirty-Eighth AIB saw its first action today near Nogent-le-Rotrou. They moved on toward Courville going through La Closure.

August 16, 1944
Courville

There was a lot of action at Courville on August 16, according to Dale. The XX Corps then moved on toward Chartres. A Company/ Thirty-Eighth AIB moved northeast of Chartres to Leves. He would tell of moving across the gently rolling French countryside and then seeing the two steeples of the great Cathedral of Chartres off in the distance come into view.

August 17-18, 1944
Chartres

On August 17, his unit was northeast of Chartres and attacked an airfield at Gasville.[14] Dale's outfit saw a lot of action around Chartres.

Fearing that the city would be bombed and shelled, the stained glass windows in the cathedral had been removed by the citizens of Chartres. The city did suffer heavy damage from bombings during World War II, but the Cathedral of Chartres was spared by an American army officer who challenged the order to destroy it. The officer went behind enemy lines to find out whether the German army was occupying the cathedral. After he returned from his reconnaissance, he reported that the cathedral was clear of enemy troops. The order to destroy the cathedral was withdrawn, and the Seventh Armored Division later liberated the area. The officer, who did the reconnaissance, was killed in action on August 16, 1944, in the town of Leves. Figure 13 is a photograph of the Seventh Armored Division memorial located on the "Esplanade de la Resistance" in Chartres.

Fig. 13. Hubley photo

Seventh Armored Memorial in Chartres

August 19-20, 1944
Dreux

On August 19, A Company/Thirty-Eighth AIB was sent to Chateauneuf and then north from there to Dreux to assist another American outfit. His unit saw a lot of action on the nineteenth fighting in Dreux. They then turned south toward Chartres the following day, August 20, 1944, to prepare for the next objective, which was an attack on Paris.

August 20-22, 1944
Dreux to Melun

After leaving Dreux, the Seventh Armored Division started toward the French capital, but as the division reached the outskirts of town, it was declared an open city, and the Seventh Armored Division, as part of the XX Corps, turned south. The American troops would not enter Paris until the Free French forces, led by Maj. Gen. Jacques LeClerc, marched in first.[15]

As the Seventh Armored Division turned south and headed toward Melun, the Germans took off in all directions. There were a lot of Germans in and around Paris and Melun. "They tried to get their troops together and stop the Americans, but they were never able. The Third Army saw to that. Patton had maybe five or six armored divisions in the area, and we kept the Germans on the run," Dale said.

On August 20, the Thirty-Eighth AIB had moved southeast of Dreux. On the twenty-first, the battalion moved through Maintenon, Bleury, Albis, and to Dourdan just south of Paris. On August 22, the Thirty-Eighth moved through Etrechy, Monceau, and Orgenoy and reached Melun.

On a road outside of Melun, Dale's unit came to a railroad underpass and stopped to look it over for mines or other booby traps. A few bodies were found, which had been blown to pieces, probably civilians taking cover when somebody stepped on a mine. Dale's captain sent two men up on the railroad tracks to see if there were Germans left behind to blow up the train trestle. Sure enough, there were two Germans with a hand-plunger detonator. The Americans killed them, and the column moved safely through the underpass and continued on to Melun.

CHAPTER 3

————◆•◆•◆————

Melun

August 23, 1944
Melun

AFTER REACHING THE SEINE River, the GIs stopped their vehicles before getting to the river and crawled up to the west riverbank. There was a sidewalk along the riverbank with a two—or three-foot-high stone wall that the men hid behind. Dale peeked over to see what they were attacking. The Germans held the east side of the river.

The following is Dale's account of the attack on the island at Melun:

> There was a lot of gunfire coming from the three—or four-story buildings across the river. Little did we know then that the building across the river was a French prison and that it was on an island in the middle of the Seine River. General Walker brought up about 6 of our tanks

to the river bankriverbank. I couldn't believe General Walker going up and down the sidewalk directing tank fire across the river. There was a lot of heavy fire back and forth across the river. The GI next to me started to peek over the wall to return fire, and a machine gun burst hit him and blew off the top of his skull. Brain matter sprayed over me.

Fig. 14. Hubley photo

Where Dale crossed the Seine River on a destroyed bridge in Melun

An aide came up to talk to General Walker. The aide was scared to death as rounds were fired back and forth across the river. He kept ducking down while talking to General Walker. General Walker never took cover but kept on walking back and forth directing fire across the river.

My platoon, 3rd Third Rifle Platoon—A Company—was ordered to cross the river on a blown bridge. The bridge was a two span with concrete supports in the center. The Germans had blown the bridge at the center support, dropping both sides into the river. That left about a four-foot opening from the riverbank to the bridge. I saw GIs getting picked off trying to jump the opening. I knew I could not swim with all my equipment, so when my turn came to go down I removed the extra ammo ammunition from my neck so I could drop the ammo and my rifle in the water, which I did.

As I jumped across the opening, I saw a lot of our GIs laying lying down there. The Germans had direct fire on that opening of the bridge. As I ran down the bridge to the water, I stepped in the water and went down like a rock. I dropped everything in my hand, but I had three hand grenades—one in my belt and two in my shoulder harness. I paddled around the center stone pier to the other half of the bridge and walked up the side to the top and peeked over and saw 2 GI's who tried to run across to a building and didn't make it. We see that in movies but not in combat. I looked over the other side of the bridge and saw another concrete support that would provide cover with steel rods sticking out of the concrete. They were about 5 feet apart, so I hung over the side and was just able to touch the first rod. I balanced myself and reached down and grabbed the rod and went down like a monkey to the next rod. The same to the next rod. Then I dropped to the ground. There were two GIs down there who had jumped off the bridge. They probably had broken legs. They told me they saw some GIs go down the path and through a hole in the wall and up the side of the river bank.

Going up the river bank, I saw a man trying to put out a fire on the roof of a big barn. One of our tanks across the river shot him. I went through the doorway of the wall wondering what to do. I saw a GI peep out of a window in a building down the block and motion to me. I ran down and jumped through the window and found five GI's in the back of a pool room. A French man was in there. We motioned to him and asked where would we would be safe? He took us back to a trap door trapdoor and we went down to a big room. There were four ladies, and one was crying so loud we knew we could not stay there. It was her husband who was shot off the roof of the barn. We talked it over. Several guys said they would look for a safer place. They found a bank building close by. We went there and went down a stairway to the basement of the bank. We forced the door open, and one of the guys agreed to swim the river and tell our tanks our location. They could protect our three sides. We could take care of the Germans coming down the steps. Half of the steps were filled with firewood for winter. The group felt since I did not have a rifle it would be better for me to lay lie on the woodpile as I had 3 hand grenades, which I did. The Germans were walking around during the night, and we could see them walk past the basement window, but nobody found us.

XX Corps was able to get more troops across in the morning and made contact with our group of 7 GIs who spent the night on the island. In the morning, we saw men walking around, but they were not German soldiers.

They wanted the GI's to give them guns and said they would help us kill the Germans. We did not give them guns; we were not sure who they were or if they were playing a trick. A little bit later, we found out about the prison on this island. The Germans let all the prisoners out and blew up the bridge to the mainland on the other side of the island. Our men put a walk bridge across, and the French prison officials came across and told us to kill all the prisoners. We said, "No, if they don't bother us." We are after the Germans. It was not long until the prisoners were gone. I think the officials rounded them up and made a deal with them. They were sure worried about what to do with them. With the bridges blown up, they [prisoners] couldn't get off the island.

August 24, 1944
Melun to Fontainebleau

Dale and the other seven or eight GIs that hid overnight on the island made contact with the American troops that crossed over to the island at 10:00 a.m. Company A / Thirty-Eighth AIB then moved south of Melun toward Fontainebleau.

August 25-26, 1944
Fontainebleau

"We were just north of Fontainebleau and were ordered to cross the Seine River and hold the other side until the engineers could put a bridge across for our tanks. There was heavy fighting about a half mile east of us. The Germans blew the bridge from each end, and it dropped in the river leaving the top rail about four feet above the water. The rail was about eight inches wide. We crawled across with rifle and ammunition. Lucky no one fell into the river," Dale said.

On the other side, a man had a shed that was full of wine bottles. The bottles were covered with wicker and had a wicker handle. He gave each one of the GIs a bottle in a nice wicker basket. "I don't think any of us drank it," Dale remembered.

Dale's unit went up a small hill next to the road and found a vineyard. They dug in and got ready for action when they saw a German half-track with soldiers coming toward the bridge. "The Germans stopped and talked to the wine man and then turned around and got the heck out of there. After waiting a while, the captain told us to return to our half-tracks. Recrossing the bridge on the small rail on top of the bridge, all that was heard were the wine bottles dropping into the river as the GIs were trying to hang on to the small beam. The wine man was taken back to HQ to be interrogated," said Dale.

CHAPTER 4

Rapid Move to Verdun

August 27-30, 1944
Fontainebleau to Reims

THE ENGINEERS PUT A bridge across the Seine north of Fontainebleau and Dale's Company A moved out on the twenty-seventh and went quickly through Hericy to Nangis. The Seventh Armored regrouped into separate task forces. At Provins, Column B included the Thirty-Eighth AIB under CCR (Combat Command Reserve).[16] On August 28, Column B moved through La Forestiere, Barbonne-Fayel and to Mareuil-en-Brie. August 29 found Dale's Company A moving through Moussy, Pierry, and through Epernay. They crossed the Marne River late in the day and moved on to an area five miles north of Reims. The next day, August 30, Company A was sent north to Rethal, passing through Tagnon. Their mission was to secure a bridge on the Aisne River.[17]

Fig. 15. Hubley photo

Seventh Armored Division monument at Nangis

American vehicles were equipped to go through water eight feet deep. The exhaust pipe and carburetor pipe were the same height. All connections were waterproof. The trouble was the tanks and vehicles ahead made the bank of the river slippery. It was hard to follow, as each vehicle in turn had the same problem. When Dale's half-track forded the river and finally made it up the bank, the vehicles in front were already out of sight; they had taken off as fast as possible. After getting to the top of the riverbank, the half-track that Dale was riding in took off down the road, but they could not see any vehicles in front of them.

He explained, "Our half-track came to a fork in the road, but we didn't know which way to go. One guy thought he saw a cloud of dust ahead so we took the road to the left. We finally came to an entrance in a grove of trees with vehicles back in the woods. We thought the vehicles were from our unit. We turned in, and two Germans stepped out of a little guard shed. They probably thought we were one of their vehicles. When they saw Americans, they started pointing we should go the other way. We didn't stop but went in behind the shed and turned around and got the heck out of there. It so surprised everyone that nobody fired a shot. The Germans were as happy to see us go as we were to go. Then we found our unit down the other fork of the road."

As the Seventh Armored moved rapidly from Fontainebleau toward Reims, Dale said the following, "An infantryman and I were walking along a road, and the Germans started shelling us. We took shelter while we were being shelled. When it stopped, the other GI and I started walking around. He had his bayonet on his rifle. All infantrymen kept their bayonets attached. I was in a bazooka squad, so we normally do not attach our bayonets. As we passed a big bush, he shoved his rifle in the bush. A German, who was hiding, yelled. We pulled the German from the bush and tried to remove the bayonet, but it was stuck in him. The GI was surprised, and his finger was still on the trigger. As the GI tried to pull the bayonet out, his finger squeezed the trigger, and he emptied his clip into the German. I had to help the GI get the bayonet out of the dead man."

"Every now and then, we passed a cornfield, and Germans would fire at us. We would hear the bullets hit the side of the half-track. The driver would turn into the cornfield, and our machine gunner would spray the corn shocks, and the Germans would jump out of the shocks with their hands up. Armored units are not equipped to take prisoners. The Germans could not use rifles in the shocks, only pistols. We had orders: Take no prisoners. Do with them what you want."

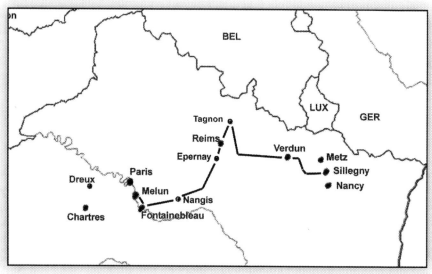

Fig. 16. Hubley map

Seventh Armored Division movement from Melun to Sillegny

The armored units were told to never take prisoners because German SS troops would put grenades in their pants and, when stripped and searched, would explode the grenades. Also, prisoners would slow down the armored units. Sometimes, Germans would be captured, but the infantry would take care of them. The Germans would be put in a large circle in the center of a field with a machine gun on each side. The prisoners were instructed to take everything out of their pockets and lay the items on the ground and then take off all their clothes. The GIs would tell the prisoners what to put on and what to put in their pockets. The prisoners would then be marched off, and the GIs would take what they wanted from what was left. GIs could get souvenirs from the Germans but had no place to keep or carry them. There were always children waiting to get what was left.

Dale said, "I was riding in the back of a half-track, and a GI was up front on the machine gun. There were seven or eight German prisoners in front of the half-track. We heard a low flying plane coming and thought it might be a German doing a strafing run. The captain in the jeep in front of the half-track yelled back to slow them [the Germans] down. The machine gunner thought he said, "Mow 'em down." He opened fire and killed the Germans. Nothing was ever said or done about the incident. It was just a mistake of war, and we won."

"Patton had, I think, four or five armored divisions working to keep the Germans from getting a fighting force together. We were on the move day and night. I think there were American armored units coming up from the south also," Dale guessed.

The Third Army was continuing its movement east of Paris toward Verdun. XX Corp was moving toward Metz, while VII Corp was centered more on Nancy to the south of Metz. The Seventh Army had landed in Southern France and was moving north toward Germany on the Third Army's right flank. The First Army was on the Third Army's left flank moving east toward the Ardennes and Belgium. The Twenty-First British Army Group under Montgomery was north of the First Army pushing toward Brussels and Antwerp.[18]

The Americans would try to disrupt German communications. "I recall seeing strips of tinfoil the planes would drop, hanging on trees and houses. The tinfoil was being used to help disrupt the German radio communication with other units," Dale said.

To prevent American pilots from strafing Allied units, different colors of banners were carried. The pilots would tell the American units what color banner to put on top of their vehicles. At one place, there was a German column moving near to Dale's position. An air strike was called in, and Dale's unit was told what color banner to use.

The fighter planes came and flew over the American columns and the German group to the south but returned to their base without firing a shot. The pilots said both columns had the same color banner, and they didn't know which column to strafe. "Thank goodness the pilots didn't shoot because the Germans had intercepted the message and were flying the same color banners!" Dale said.

By the end of August 1944, the XX Corps had become known as the Ghost Corps. Maj. Gen. Walton H. Walker, commander of XX Corps, was a hard-driving commander similar to General Patton. The German army was never able to get a fix on where the corps was located. General Walker used speed of attack, wide-flanking movements, and cutting off German supply lines by encircling and attacking from the rear, to keep the Germans retreating and unable to locate the corps.

> The secrecy which for weeks has surrounded the mysterious "Ghost" Corps was lifted today revealing Major General Walton H. Walker's XX Corps as the spearhead of Lt. Gen. George S. Patton's Third Army's great Eastward drive across France, distinguished by bold tactics of encirclement which won Prime Minister Churchill's praise in Parliament the other day. (Joseph Driscoll in the *New York Herald Tribune*, Sept. 30, 1944)[19]

After the war, General Patton sent a letter praising General Walker. Part of the letter Patton sent said, "From the landing of the XX Corps in England until the termination of hostilities in Europe, you and your Corps have been outstanding for dash, drive, and audacity in pursuit and in exploitation. Of all the Corps I have commanded, yours has always been the most eager to attack and the most reasonable and cooperative."[20]

If an outfit's esprit de corps can be judged by its combat efficiency, the appearance and military manner of its personnel, its self-pride and confidence, then XX Corps will be satisfied with nothing but top position on the roster of US Army units serving overseas or at home.[21]

Unfortunately, by the end of August, gasoline supplies were being sent north to the US First Army and to Montgomery's Twenty-First Army Group. Patton's Third Army was facing critical gasoline shortages.

CHAPTER 5

Red Ball Express

D ALE WAS ALWAYS INTRIGUED by the Red Ball Express and what it was able to accomplish. This is a brief summary of its operations in France during World War II, taken from an article in the Quartermaster Professional Bulletin, Spring 1989.

The Red Ball Express was an enormous truck convoy system created by Allied forces to supply their forward-area combat units moving quickly through Europe following the breakout from the D-Day beaches in Normandy. The Red Ball Express used a fleet of over six thousand trucks and trailers that delivered over 412,000 tons of ammunition, food, and fuel to the Allied armies in France between August 25 and November 16, 1944.

In order to keep the supplies flowing, two routes were opened from Cherbourg to the forward logistics base at Chartres. The northern route was used for delivering supplies, the southern for returning trucks. Both roads were one way only and closed to civilian traffic. Trucks carried supplies twenty-four hours a day.

The system lasted only three months, from August 25 to November 16, 1944, until the port facilities at Antwerp, Belgium, were opened, some French rail lines were repaired, and portable gasoline pipelines were deployed.

The breakout from Normandy finally occurred the last week of July. First and Third armies joined forces on August 1 to form the US Twelfth Army Group and, at once, began their rapid movement across France.

The Germans offered even lighter resistance than expected, and Patton's Third Army burned up an average of more than 380,000 gallons of gasoline per day. By August 7 (a week after becoming operational), its reserves were completely exhausted. Patton had to rely on daily truckloads of packaged petroleum, oil, and lubricants (POL) from the rear. Nevertheless, he managed to continue this highly mobile type of warfare, driving eastward for another three weeks before being halted by critical shortages of gasoline.

The First and Third armies were simultaneously engaged in rapid pursuit across France. They consumed more gasoline during this one week, August 20-26, than any time previously. Average consumption was well over eight hundred thousand gallons per day. The First Army alone used 782,000 gallons of motor fuel on August 24.

Once across the Seine, forward divisions not only extended their lines but fanned out in every direction, creating a front twice as broad as previously planned. Believing victory to be firmly within their grasp, the fast-moving armies had outrun their supply lines and were forced to live hand-to-mouth for several days. Ninety to ninety-five percent of all supplies on the continent still lay in base depots in the vicinity of Normandy. Patton's Third Army had, in effect, advanced more than three hundred miles from Omaha beach in three weeks. The First Army had done likewise. With the situation becoming more critical daily, the Red Ball Express was born.

In late August, Eisenhower decided to forward most petroleum supplies to the First Army (Hodges) and the British Twenty-First Army Group (Montgomery). This was Montgomery's plan known as Operation Market Garden. The end result of Market Garden was that it used up many supplies, destroyed a lot of equipment, and many men were killed. It failed to achieve Montgomery's goals. This action was to come at the expense of Patton's Third Army to the South. On August 31, Patton's daily allotment of gasoline dropped off sharply from four hundred thousand to thirty-one thousand gallons. This placed a virtual stranglehold on the fiery commander, who fumed, pleaded, begged, bellowed, and cursed accordingly—but to no avail. "My men can eat their belts," he was overheard telling Ike at a meeting on September 2, "but my tanks gotta have gas." The logistical crisis threatened to halt the Allies where the enemy could not. Patton had been halted near Verdun. Patton knew Eisenhower had made a mistake in supporting Montgomery's plan instead of allowing the Third Army to continue to attack the retreating Germans.

By the end of the first week in September, consumption rates were once again hitting the eight-hundred-thousand-gallon-a-day mark. Patton's gasoline woes ended almost as quickly as they had begun. Mid-September saw the two American armies issuing in excess of one million gallons of gasoline daily—enough to meet the immediate needs and to begin building slight reserves.

Finally, the Red Ball Express had an inherent problem in that it was fast approaching a point of diminishing returns. As the route got longer and longer, the Red Ball trucks required more gasoline—ultimately as much as three hundred thousand gallons per day—just to keep the Red Ball vehicles themselves moving.[22]

CHAPTER 6

Attack on Sillegny

August 31-September 5, 1944
Verdun

ON AUGUST 31, THE Thirty-Eighth Armored Infantry Battalion was assigned to CCR (Combat Command Reserve). The battalion moved from Rethal toward Verdun. Shortly after noon on August 31, the Meuse River was crossed at Verdun. The city had been liberated by the Seventh Armored Division without inflicting any casualties on the civilian population.[23] September 1 found the Thirty-Eighth AIB at Fromezey, France—the farthest east of any American unit.[24]

At Verdun, the Seventh Armored Division was told to go across the Meuse River and dig in because they were out of gas. A lot of units were dug in to the south. Each night about 9:00 p.m., a high-flying German plane would come from the north and drop three flare bombs that were about as bright as day. The bombers were right behind and dropped their bombs on the US positions.

"Our vehicles were covered with limbs cut from trees. The GIs dug foxholes, and each day we dug them deeper. It was about five or six days later, after getting gasoline, when we started to move toward Metz," said Dale. "After taking Verdun, three or four GIs were sent out to scout Metz. They never returned. Metz was like a German West Point. It was heavily fortified. The Germans had taken many people from Verdun and made them slave labor to fortify Metz." Although several hundred civilians had been drafted by the Germans in July of 1944, they lacked equipment and supplies; therefore, very little was accomplished in fortifying the defenses.

The gas shortage had stopped Patton in his tracks. There was discussion about the reason for the shortage. While it is true that the supply lines were stretched to the limit, there were supplies, and Eisenhower decided to divert gas north to Montgomery's Twenty-First Army Group. Dale always thought that Eisenhower's decision was more political than military so that Montgomery could also get some press time the way Patton had during his dash across France. Could the war have ended sooner if Patton had been able to continue his pursuit of the fleeing Germans? One thing is certain: General Montgomery's plan was a failure. It not only failed to encircle and trap the Germans, it also failed in that it lost and wasted thousands of tons of supplies that could have been used by other armies (especially the Third Army) to continue their successful attacks. Because none of the plans were accomplished, it was also a waste of many soldiers' lives. Lastly, it caused unnecessary destruction in the Netherlands. After it was all over, Prince Bernard of the Netherlands said, "My country can never again afford the luxury of another Montgomery success."[25] The gas shortage had given the German army time to move up troops and to reinforce a line east of the Moselle River.

September 6, 1944
Haudiomont

The last entry on Dale's helmet card is Haudiomont on September 6, 1944. On September 5 or 6, Third Rifle Platoon / Company A (Dale's unit) was assigned to Seventh Armored Division guard duty. The Thirty-Eighth Armored Infantry Battalion was heavily involved in the fighting to cross the Moselle River and take Metz. The division HQ was under fairly constant artillery attacks and night bombing from German planes. Because of this, the HQ was moved every few days. From September 5 to 16, the division HQ was moved from Regret, France, to Pintheville, Mars-la-Tour, Doncourt, Sponville, Puxieux, and to Arry.[26]

September 7-17, 1944
East of Verdun

At the beginning of September, XX Corp was fighting to cross the Moselle River and encircle Metz. Weather was bad with rain and clouds that made armor movements difficult and prevented air cover much of the time. The average monthly precipitation during September, October, and November in the Lorraine area was 2.4-3.0 inches. In the autumn of 1944, the rainfall was two and three times the amount usually recorded with almost seven inches of rain in November alone.[27]

Another problem was that existing aerial photographs were up to four years old and not much was known about the fortifications around Metz and along the Moselle River. Camouflage was excellent in this area, and natural growth during the four years of German occupation enhanced the concealment.[28]

The Americans began the attack to cross the Moselle on September 6 and 7. Because of heavy German fire, the attack turned south to force a crossing at Dornot. A small tentative bridgehead was established at Dornot, but by September 10, the Americans were pushed back across the Moselle. About two and a half miles south of Dornot, at Arnaville, a second assault crossing was scheduled for September 10. This crossing in boats was successful, and bridging operations were started the night of September 10. It would be the first time smoke-screen operations were used to hide American troop movements. The bridge was completed on September 12 with a second bridge completed on September 14.[29]

The fighting to secure this bridgehead on the east side of the Moselle was intense, and there were heavy losses to both the Germans and Americans. This area was well defended with German artillery and infantry. On September 16, CCR began an attack to break out to the east along the Lorry-Sillegny road. The Germans were well dug in and had accurate artillery fire on the Americans as they advanced from the Moselle toward Sillegny.[30]

September 18, 1944 (Afternoon)
Arnaville Area

The attack on Sillegny was not proceeding well for the Americans, and because of heavy losses, more reinforcements were needed. Thus, Company A was removed from division guard duty and moved to the front to support the attack on Sillegny.

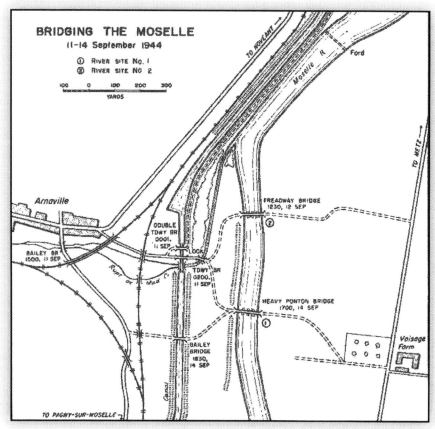

Fig. 17. Three Battles: Arnaville, Altuzzo, and Schmidt

Diagram of the crossing sites at Arnaville

Dale's Third Rifle Platoon went south of Metz and crossed the Moselle River at Arnaville to try to circle Metz. He continued, "The GIs put up two pontoon bridges to get across the river. A GI unit was operating smoke machines which covered the valley and the two bridges which we crossed. We heard bombs exploding, but the Germans could not find us and destroy the bridges."

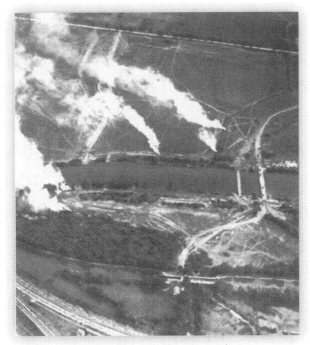

Fig. 18. The Lorraine Campaign

Smoke being used to cover the crossing site at Arnaville

September 18, 1944 (Evening)
West of Sillegny (In the Woods)

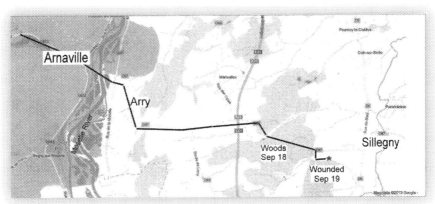

Fig. 19. Base map Google

Arnaville to Sillegny

The Third Rifle Platoon went through some small towns and then into a forest west of Sillegny. The US Army set up machine guns to prevent a German counterattack. Dale continued the account, "It was night, and we were on a dark road in thick woods. Americans were walking single file when a German threw a hand grenade. There were approximately five hundred German SS troops in the woods this night. The Americans scattered and jumped into ditches on both sides of the road. In the dark, you could not tell who was an American or where the Germans were. All was quiet. Then somebody fell and landed on top of me. I don't know if he is a German or an American. Then the guy started to say "pssst." A second man returned the call "pssst" and moved close to where I was lying. The man on top of me told his buddy, 'I'm lying on a stiff.' I knew now that he was American, and I said, 'Like hell you are!' Scared the hell out of the man on top of me, but he stayed there, and I was glad for that because he protected me. We could not even see the jeeps as they moved up the road to pick up the injured. Later, we moved back down the road where the jeeps had come from. We found small German bunkers that two men could fit in with their head at the opening giving them a field of view to cover. A sergeant was checking the men, and a GI shot him. The GI thought he was a German approaching. Everyone was tense and on edge."

Fig. 20. Hubley photo

German bunkers in the woods

September 19, 1944
Sillegny

Through the morning of September 19, a confused and bloody battle continued at the edge of Sillegny. To get some idea of the intensity of the battle, consider that this day, September 19, at the start of the day Lt. Col. William W. Rosebro was the commanding officer of the Thirty-Eighth Armored Infantry Battalion. He died of wounds from a bullet through the forehead. Maj. Curtice H. Rankin was made the CO of the Thirty-Eighth AIB but was killed by a mortar shell. The next CO was Maj. Thomas H. Wells. He was killed by a 150 mm shell. Lt. Col. Ted King was assigned as CO but was wounded and evacuated. Lt. Col. Robert L. Rhea survived until September 20 and then replaced by Lt. Col. William H. G.

Fuller. On September 19, three different commanding officers were killed in action, and one was wounded. The fierce fighting was why Company A was rushed up to the frontline from its post as division headquarters guard.

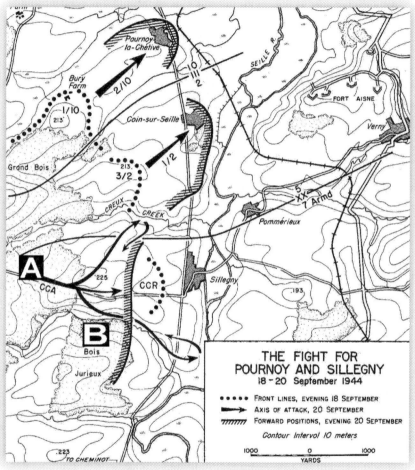

Fig. 21. The Lorraine Campaign

Dale in the woods overnight—(A) Wounded—(B)

Dale's group assembled in the morning and left the woods to attack Sillegny. During an attack, the infantry soldiers would follow a tank for protection. As the GIs were walking behind the tank, they would throw grenades into German dug-in positions. But not all the Germans were killed, and they started firing from behind. Dale's outfit came out of the woods and moved south along a tree line toward Sillegny. The enemy artillery and tank fire was intense, and at 1100 hours, Lt. Col. Ted King gave orders to withdraw the assault companies. The tank driver got his orders to retreat and yelled, "I'm backing up," and put the tank in reverse. Dale turned around to get out of the way of the tank and just remembered dirt coming up into his face from an artillery shell explosion. He thought someone pulled him out of the way of the tank.

Dale continued, "I am not sure if the tank ran over me or someone pulled me out of the way. I don't know how much clearance between the bottom of the tank and the road. I don't know how long I lay there. When I came to, it was quiet, and all the vehicles and GIs were gone except one tank. I raised my head a little, and someone took a shot at me. I knew I was not alone."

When Dale came to after being shelled, his mind was sharp. When he lifted his head, he could hear the bullet snap as it went over. Dale did not know where his unit was or where the German line was. He knew that when the shell exploded, his unit was pulling back, and he did not know if the Germans had overrun his position. He wondered if he was now behind the German line.

Dale said, "When I came to, things looked so different—a disabled tank was over to my right. No one was around, but the BBC news was on the radio. After being shot at, I peeked up under my helmet liner to see how I could get to the nearby woods. I saw somebody look up and motion me with his finger. I was not sure who he was. I then looked over to my left and saw a small rain ditch by the woods. If I could crawl like a snake over to the low part, I'd be okay, which is what I did. When I got to the edge of the woods,

I rolled down into a deep shell hole, and two GIs were standing up in the hole. It probably was ten feet deep. I could tell they were not normal, and I tried to get them to follow me when I ran out into the woods about twenty yards away. I lay down and called to them, but no answer. The German artillery was shelling up and down the edge of the woods. I knew I could not wait on the GIs, so I ran another fifteen or twenty yards, stopped, and called again—but no response. No one shot at me, so I felt maybe I was not in enemy grounds. I lowered my rifle so I would not shoot it at anyone. Still, I felt I was walking into a German trap."

Fig. 22. US Army photo

Reconnaissance photo of Sillegny

A problem was that Germans were taking American GI uniforms and posing as Americans. Also, Dale was not sure if the American lines were in front or behind him.

Dale said, "I kept going in a straight direction. Finally, I saw a camouflaged soldier lying on the ground with a machine gun pointed at me. I kept my rifle lowered at my side and walked straight at the machine gun. He was hiding in the weeds, and I could not tell if he was American or German. I hoped that by not raising my rifle he wouldn't feel threatened.

"He said, 'Halt, what is the password?' I told him our outfit left before we got the password but I'd tell him yesterday's password. He said, 'No good.' He asked me what outfit I was in. I told him. He said, 'I never heard of it.' He asked, 'Where did you live?' I said, 'Cincinnati.' He said, 'That town does not have a good ball team.' I said, 'We have a good team—the Cincinnati Reds.' We started talking about the Reds, their players and team statistics. We talked about what league the Reds were in, their win/loss record, and the town of Cincinnati. We convinced each other that we were both Americans because no German would know all those details about the Reds. Then we were sure we were on the same side. Come to find out, the GI behind the machine gun was from Covington, Kentucky, just across the river from Cincinnati. I told him about the two GIs in the shell hole. He said they brought up the engineers and anyone else who could shoot a gun to help take the town."

Fig. 23. Cincinnati Reds

Needless to say, Dale was a lifelong Cincinnati Reds fan!

"The GI told me where the American units were. I started that way when a tank with an officer came down the road toward me, stopped, and asked where I was going. The officer said, 'Turn around and follow me because we are getting a fighting force together,' then the tank continued on toward Sillegny. I followed until he was out of sight then turned around and went the opposite way where I finally found one of our half-tracks." The second attack on Sillegny began at one-fifteen in the afternoon, but Dale would not see any more combat.

Lt. Col. King was wounded during the second attack on Sillegny, and Lt. Col. Robert Rhea assumed command. There was fierce fighting all day with heavy losses on both sides. By seven in the evening, Lt. Col. Rhea broke off the engagement. A number of the CCR staff were killed or wounded. The Thirty-Eighth Armored Infantry Battalion had been reduced to about one-fourth its normal strength, and most of its officers were dead. General Silvester, XX Corps commander, ordered CCA to relieve CCR, and on the following morning, the badly shattered reserve command withdrew into the woods.[32]

September 20, 1944
Nancy

Dale did not have much use of his right arm, so he was sent to a field hospital near Nancy. At the field hospital, a day or so later, the doctor asked him how he felt. Dale said, "Good." The doctor asked if he felt okay to return to his unit. Dale answered, "Yes." Then the doctor saw his age on the chart and said, "What the hell are they sending you old men over here for! I'm sending you to P2."

"I didn't know what that was, so I asked the nurse what it meant." She said, 'You're lucky, you are going back to England.'

"I was sure happy. The next day, a small four-seat plane took me to Paris."

Fig. 24. Hubley photo

Monument in Sillegny dedicated to the Seventh Armored Division

The battle for Sillegny, Metz, and on to the Saar River continued until December 19. On September 20, the Thirty-Eighth AIB was estimated to be down to one-quarter strength. By September 24, the Thirty-Eighth Armored Infantry Battalion was declared to be no longer an effective fighting force because of all the causalities and was pulled out of combat. It bivouacked back across the Moselle River at Puxieux. On September 25, the Seventh Armored Division, which included the Thirty-Eighth Armored Infantry Battalion, was assigned to the First Army and began a march to Belgium to get replacements, equipment, and retraining.[33]

The Germans had removed all civilians from the town of Sillegny before the Americans reached the area. They then laid minefields in the open ground to the west of town. The wide-open ground around Sillegny meant that the battlefield was not in control of either side most of the time. The battle for Sillegny went on for a month. Even when the town was secured in mid—to late October 1944, the absence of civilians and the presence of the German minefields meant that American and German bodies were not recovered for a year and a half until de-mining operations could take place.

After three months of fighting (Sept. 1-Dec. 19, 1944) the Third Army sustained 55,182 combat casualties during the Lorraine Campaign (6,657 KIA; 36,406 WIA; 12,119 MIA).[34] Exact German losses in Lorraine were unknown but were suspected to be severe. At least seventy-five thousand German prisoners were captured by the Third Army during the offensive.[35] Offensive operations by the US Army in this part of the Western Front did not resume until mid-March 1945 with the objective of occupying the Saar-Palatinate.

CHAPTER 7

Back to England

Late September 1944
Paris

AT PARIS, A SCHOOLHOUSE was being used for the hospital. Dale remembered, "A GI had shot himself in the hand so that he would get sent home. He was supposed to get penicillin but did not show the nurse his ID sheet. I told the nurse. The nurse was mad and came in all night to wake the guy up and give him his shots."

A few days later, they put Dale on a C-47 supply plane and flew him to Newbury, England. He said, "I knew I was on my way home sometime in the future."

Late September 1944
Newbury, England

After being shelled, Dale had been flown from Nancy to Paris, then Paris to Newbury, England, near London. On the plane to Newbury, guys were getting sick, and a bucket was passed up and down the aisle. Some of the guys that got sick were paratroopers. After landing in Newbury, Dale was hospitalized.

At the hospital, a GI showed Dale where to slip out through a hole in the fence and go to a small town nearby. "The GI was a little on the wild side," Dale said. He continued, "You could catch the bus right outside. I think the hole in the fence was put there on purpose. I saw GIs real sick, and they wanted to see a doctor. But they had a rule: unless you had a fever of one hundred degrees or higher, the nurse would only bring several aspirin, and that was it. The GIs would get mad, put their clothes on, go out the hole in the fence, catch the bus, go to town, and sit in a pub and drink beer. They would come back to the hospital, and the next morning, they were a lot better—ready to go again. That's all they needed!"

From the beginning of September 1944 until the end of November 1944, no information about Dale reached his wife. For almost three months, she had not heard from him. Then a Red Cross nurse took this picture of Dale toward the end of November and sent it to Wanda to show that he was okay and back in England. What a relief for Wanda! Although Dale would talk about his war experiences, he never said much about this period of time that he was in the hospital. Wanda would say that she could tell by looking at Dale's picture that he had been through a tough time.

Fig. 25. Hubley photo

Nov. 1944 photo taken by a Red Cross nurse

December 1944-September 1945
Newbury, England

After being released from the hospital, Dale was assigned to the 994th Ordnance Heavy Automotive Maintenance Company where he took a course to be classified as an automotive mechanic. After about four months, his grade was a Tech/5, and his principal duty was as a clerk-general. He performed general clerical work such as preparing inventory cards and requisitions.

The 994th HAM Co. was repairing vehicles to be shipped to Japan. The war in Japan was not over yet, and they needed vehicles. There was a German prison camp about one half mile away from the base in Newbury. The German POWs would be marched up each day to do all the work. Dale was put in charge of the parts department and had two German prisoners working for him; one spoke English. They would go to the different departments and see what parts were needed. If they needed a certain part, Dale would take his jeep and go to a big field about two or three miles away where vehicles were brought to be stored. Guards at the entrance would check every one in and out. The jeeps, trucks, and other vehicles were stored in separate places. At the gate, they checked Dale's vehicle to be sure he came out in the same vehicle.

Dale continued, "An officer would ask me if I could get him a better jeep as his was not working so well. I would take his jeep down to the field. The guards would check me in, and I knew where the jeeps were—a long way from the guards. I would take off the hood where the numbers were stenciled and find a good jeep and exchange hoods. I still had the same numbered jeep when I came out (at least the guards thought so). I was not allowed to take a German prisoner with me when I would go for parts or vehicles."

As the camps in England were being closed down, they would send all their unit bicycles, vehicles, and supplies to this big camp at Newbury. There was an eight-foot fence around the camp. Hundreds of bicycles were brought in and stored four or five high along a part of the fence. Civilians would pass by and were mad about all the bikes the Americans had in junk storage. The civilian people were badly in need of bicycles and wanted to buy them, but London wanted to get their production of bicycles going again. So the civilians complained to London Headquarters, and the Americans agreed to an inspection of the camp. The inspection team didn't see a bike. All the bicycles were covered with tarps. When the inspectors drove through, they did not see a bike!

Later, some of the good bikes were sent to Germany for the GIs stationed there. The rest were cut up for scrap. Dale made a bike with a jeep battery and jeep headlight to ride at night into London. It gets dark in London in the winter about 4:30 p.m. In the summer, it stays light till about 10:30 or 11:00 p.m.

Toward the end of summer 1945, as bases were closing, Dale was told to bury all jeep and truck parts. He knew a mechanic at a garage and asked the mechanic if he wanted the parts. He said yes. So Dale filled up a ton-and-a-half truck with stuff and dumped it in this guy's lot. Dale said, "The man was scared to death he would be found with all this US stuff! We were starting to close the base, and they told us to bury all the parts. I hope I did the right thing, giving that equipment to him."

CHAPTER 8

---•◆•---

Home

September 1945
England to USA

"ON 13 SEPTEMBER 1945, an orderly found me in another part of camp and told me to get packed to leave tomorrow to go home. I threw my bike in the jeep and left for the barracks. I have always been sorry I did not say good-bye to the two men working for me and get their address. I wonder whatever happened to them. The next day, I fell in with others who were picked to go home. We got in GM trucks and started for Southampton to catch a boat. We stopped at a camp near Swindon for five days. Then we left C-18 for Southampton. It was a one-night-two-day trip. The *Queen Mary* and several other liners were ready to load. Two days later, they lined us up in front of the *Queen Mary*, and I was happy to ride her again," Dale remembered.

Dale boarded the *Queen Mary* in Southampton at 6:30 a.m. on September 23, 1945. She sailed at 1:00 p.m. It was Voyage 54W for the *Queen*. There were 14,938 troops on board, and it took four days, twenty hours, forty minutes to cross the Atlantic. The *Queen Mary* arrived in New York at noon on September 28, 1945.[36]

Dale remembered, "It was a wonderful ride back to New York. When we landed, we opened the little round window and looked out. A small band was playing, and a girl on crutches named Jane Froman, a well-known singer at that time, was singing as the GIs were getting off the boat. She had been in an airplane accident. On the wharf, there were several ladies handing out a carton of milk to each GI. I'll never forget how good it was after drinking powdered milk for about two years.

"We took a train to Camp Kilmer in New Jersey. They gave us a royal dinner, steaks and all the trimmings. They processed us, and the next day, September 29 at 9:00 p.m., we said good-bye to our friends, and we took off in all directions. I arrived at Camp Atterbury in Indiana on September 30. I was again processed and was discharged Tuesday morning, October 2, 1945.

"I caught a train for Ohio coming through Greenville, Ohio. I called Wanda, and she, Alan, Wanda's sister, Dorothy, and her daughter, Heidi, met me. That was wonderful. Wanda was living in Celina at that time. When I went in the house, I dumped my duffel bag on the floor, and the kids had a good time going through it."

A Mother's Poems

These two poems were written by Dale's mother, Estella Mae Rankin Hubley. She wrote the poems while her son was serving in World War II. The "Stars in the Window Panes" refers to the blue or gold stars that families of those who were overseas fighting would place in a front window of their homes. A blue star indicated that your loved one is currently serving. The gold star indicated an armed service member was killed or missing in action during the war.

To Our Service Men and Service Women

The emblem of his service true,
Is the star of promise,
Just as the stars above,
Are peeking through
The reminders of heaven.

Today we see the stars
Of service men and women
Teeming through the window panes
Of homes in memory of loved ones
In service for our country.

It matters not what race or creed
Sacrificing for our country's need.
They are God's children be it understood
Serving in one grand brotherhood.

Be it on land, sea, or air
In the hour of need they are there.

Under the Folds

Under the folds of the red, the white, and the blue
We are thinking of you.
While you are protecting our U. S. of A.
Although be many miles away.

Under the folds of the flag
All people are at liberty to do right.
Let no one his duty flag
While our brave soldiers fight.

Five-point service for the star
Wave their folds ever near and far.
Each stripe of the red and the white
Our emblem of Liberty, Peace, and Right.

General Patton's Letter

The following is a letter General Patton sent to the troops at the end of the war.

HEADQUARTERS
THIRD UNITED STATES ARMY
APO 403

GENERAL ORDERS   19 MAY 1945
NUMBER 98

SOLDIERS OF THE THIRD ARMY,
PAST AND PRESENT

During the 281 days of incessant and victorious combat, your penetrations have advanced farther in less time than any other army in history. You have fought your way across 24 major rivers and innumerable lesser streams. You have liberated or conquered more than 82,000 square miles of territory, including 1500 cities and towns, and some 12,000 inhabited places. Prior to the termination of active hostilities, you had captured in battle 956,000 enemy soldiers and killed or wounded at least 500,000 others. France, Belgium, Luxemburg, Germany, Austria, and Czechoslovakia bear witness to your exploits.

All men and women of the six corps and thirty-nine divisions that have at different times been members of this Army have done their duty. Each deserves credit. The enduring valor of the combat troops has been paralleled and made possible by the often unpublicized activities of the supply, administrative and medical services of this Army and of the Communications Zone troops supporting it. Nor should we forget our comrades of the other armies and of the Air Force, particularly of the XIX Tactical Air Command by whose side or under whose wings we have had the honor to fight.

In proudly contemplating our achievements, let us never forget our heroic dead whose graves mark the course of our victorious advances, nor our wounded whose sacrifices aided so much to our success.

I should be both ungrateful and wanting in candor if I failed to acknowledge the debt we owe to our Chiefs of Staff, Generals Gaffey and Gay, and to the officers and men of the General and Special Staff Sections of Army Headquarters. Without their loyalty, intelligence, and unremitting labors, success would have been impossible.

The termination of fighting in Europe does not remove the opportunities for other outstanding and equally difficult achievements in the days which are to come. In some ways the immediate future will demand of you more fortitude than has the past because without the inspiration of combat, you must maintain—by your dress, deportment, and efficiency—not only the prestige of the Third Army, but also the honor of the United States. I have complete confidence that you will not fail.

During the course of this war I have received promotions and decorations far above and beyond my individual merit. You won them; I as your representative wear them. The one honor which is mine and mine alone is that of having commanded such an incomparable group of Americans, the record of whose fortitude, audacity, and valor will endure as long as history lasts.

G. S. PATTON JR.
General[37]

1945-1997

Dale found when he returned home to Cincinnati, Ohio, that many of his friends who were in their late thirties and early forties who had not been drafted had been able to stay at their jobs and had moved up in both salary and position. He also realized that some of his friends had taken jobs in war production industries to avoid being drafted. Because of this, Dale and Wanda moved to Mount Washington, a suburb in Cincinnati, for a change of location. In 1947, their second son, Roger, was born. By 1949, Dale realized that rather than stay in Cincinnati and feel that he no longer fit in with his old friends, he and Wanda would move. They moved to a small town just south and west of Cleveland called North Eaton.

Dale landed a good job at the Chevrolet plant in Brookpark near Cleveland and became a foreman in the transmission assembly section. Everything again seemed to be going well for the family until the winter of 1953-54 when both Dale and Roger came down with pneumonia and were hospitalized. The doctor said that because of the damp air around Lake Erie in northern Ohio, the family should move to a drier climate. So Dale, rather than moan and groan about moving again, bought a large truck, packed up their belongings, and moved the family to Denver, Colorado.

The truck was a twenty—or twenty-four-foot enclosed truck similar to today's U-Haul trucks. Dale also had a twelve-foot trailer that he loaded, and Wanda pulled it behind the car. Dale and one of the boys would lead, and Wanda with the other boy would follow. The truck also had a flat extension on the back that was packed full. The trailer had two tarps tied down, covering everything that was piled on the trailer. Think *The Beverly Hillbillies!*

The family left North Eaton and drove to Wanda's sister's farm the farm of Wanda's sister just outside of Lima, Ohio. It was February, and when they went to leave the next morning, the truck would not start. Dale and his brother-in-law spent most of the day trying to thaw out the gas line and work on the radiator and carburetor. There is one thing they did not check. The truck was out of gas.

The following morning, with gas, the family headed to Denver. They had only gone about one hundred miles and were just across the Indiana state line when a large semitrailer truck started to pass and pulled next to Wanda. But he did not pass her. Instead, he slowed down and pulled back behind Wanda. The semi driver did this three more times, and Wanda was scared to death. She thought the driver was flirting with her, and she was afraid to look at him as he tried to pass. Dale was watching all this in his rearview mirror. Finally, the truck driver passed Wanda and pulled beside Dale. The semi driver had figured out Dale and Wanda were probably traveling together and yelled at Dale, "That lady behind you has been driving with a flat tire on the trailer for more than ten miles!" So they covered about one hundred miles that day and stopped to find a new tire for the trailer.

They followed US Route 36 from Indianapolis all the way to Denver. Remember, there were no interstates. Dale and Wanda agreed that if they got separated, she would stay on the east side of any major bridge, and Dale would circle around and find her. During a snowstorm in Hannibal, Missouri, they became separated. Dale thought that Wanda got lost going through the downtown and searched for over two hours. Finally, he went back across the Mississippi River and found Roger and her waiting on the side of the road before crossing the bridge.

At St. Joseph, Missouri, the family stayed in an old downtown hotel. Alan and Roger went exploring and saw a red pipe going from the floor to ceiling with a wood handle attached. Alan pulled the wood handle and set off the fire alarm. It was probably twenty degrees outside, and all the guests got to go outside unexpectedly. Dale never got mad at the boys. I think he realized if he were a young boy, he would have pulled the handle also.

Traveling west on US Route 36, the Rocky Mountains finally came into view. Dale and Wanda stopped, and they all got out to view the snowcapped mountains in the distance. Everyone, especially the boys, was excited. Denver, mountains, wide open spaces, and cowboys! What more could two boys ask for.

But jobs were hard to find in Denver, and Dale was unable to find work. Wanda was extremely homesick, and the two boys had been out of school for six weeks. So Dale bought three train tickets and sent Wanda and the boys back to Ohio where they could stay with Wanda's sister. He drove the truck to Ohio then went back to Denver on the train and drove the car back.

Alan and Roger started school, but Roger had problems and did not want to go to school. At first, the school was not sure what grade he should be in. All he could tell the principal was that his grade card was on the truck, and the principal could not figure that one out. Two good things came from Roger meeting with the principal. Whatever the principal said worked because Roger had no more problems going to school. Second, the principal found out that Roger's mom had been a second grade teacher and he needed an elementary teacher.

The family bought a house in Spencerville, Ohio, which was close to four of Wanda's siblings. Dale found a job with Peterson Construction Company; Wanda started teaching first grade, and the boys settled in to school.

In 1977, after he had retired from Peterson Construction Company and Wanda retired from teaching, they sold their home and most of their belongings and moved to Santa Rosa, California, to be near Alan and their grandkids. Years later, they moved to Phoenix, Arizona, to help out Wanda's oldest sister. When Dale and Wanda were in their mid-eighties, they moved again, this time to Celina, Ohio, where they rented half of a two-family condo.

There was one time when both boys were visiting their parents in Celina that Dale and Wanda thought they should all go to a funeral home and make final arrangements so no one would have to pay or make any decision when the time came. After the four of them met with the funeral director, Alan's wife remarked that "it was nice to see the family doing something together." They all had a good chuckle about that.

The nursing home where they both ended up living was directly across from a funeral home. Dale always called it corpse crossing. Even after he could no longer use his legs, whenever you visited him, he would say, "When I get out of here, we will go play golf." He knew he would not walk again, but he never lost his sense of humor.

Dale and Wanda had been married for sixty-two years when Dale died in 1997. Wanda passed away in 2003. No one ever heard Dale say anything negative about any of the events that shaped his life. He always had a positive attitude and never felt sorry for himself. Nothing much ever bothered him. Dale's experiences during the war shaped his outlook for the rest of his life:

I was one of the lucky ones—I got to come home.

Fig. 26. Hubley photo

Dale and Wanda in 1977

EPILOGUE

Sillegny 2013

M Y WIFE, MELODY, AND I traveled to France for two weeks in 2012 and again for two weeks in 2013 to trace my father's route in World War II. Although we went sightseeing in many large cities such as Paris, Chartres, and Melun, it was following Dad's route through the many small towns and villages that we enjoyed the most. The highlight of the four weeks spent in France was the town of Sillegny where my father was wounded.

The night before going to Sillegny, we stayed in Metz. The next morning, we drove along the Moselle River to see where the Seventh Armored Division crossed the river at Arnaville. We drove through Arry and Lorry-Mardigny, towns that Dad passed through, and then into the woods where the GIs were attacked during the night of September 18, 1944. Unexpectedly, little did I know that many of the German bunkers were still there. They were small, concrete, two-man bunkers that had a line of fire on the road passing through the woods. This was an exciting find for me because I did not know the bunkers still existed. I knew now exactly where the attack took place, and I could visualize where Dad lay flat in the ditch alongside the road as the Germans threw hand grenades.

Continuing along the D67 road out of the woods, we saw the field and the small stream where the Thirty-Eighth Armored Infantry Battalion had advanced on the morning of September 19, 1944. This was the field where my father was wounded, and it was very moving to see this area.

We drove on into town to see the monument that is dedicated to the Seventh Armored Division for liberating Sillegny. I wanted to get a picture of the monument, and then I assumed we would continue our trip and drive on to Nancy. But fate has a way of changing your plans.

As we drove into Sillegny, Melody and I had seen dozens of people hiking in the countryside. When we found the monument in the center of town at the town square, we saw that a festival was taking place. It was a holiday, and the town was hosting a cancer walkathon. So we decided to stop and check out what was going on. There was a lady and a gentleman sitting at a table selling tickets for the noon meal. Before leaving the USA, I typed up a paragraph explaining the purpose of my trip and had it translated into French. I handed the lady the paper; she read it then showed it to the man sitting with her. Neither spoke English, but we could tell that the lady wanted to show us her church that was next to the town square. The church was one of a few buildings not destroyed in September of 1944. Inside, the walls and ceiling were covered with frescoes painted in the sixteenth century. It was beautiful. Meanwhile, the man at the table had contacted Jean-Marc Grunfelder, the assistant mayor, about our visit. Jean-Marc greeted Melody and me as we came out of the church. He spoke English and asked about our trip and my dad's story. Jean-Marc said he wanted us to meet a few people and asked if we could meet him in about forty-five minutes. We said yes and used the time to walk around Sillegny. The homes were clean and well taken care of. Most had flower gardens, and many had neatly manicured vegetable gardens. We could tell that the residents of Sillegny took pride in their village of about four hundred people.

When we returned to the town square at noon, Jean-Marc was there with his wife and introduced us to Mayor Francois Lespagnol. The mayor presented us with gifts commemorating the 2009 dedication of the Seventh Armored Division monument. Jean-Marc introduced us to Jean-Marc Tabard, the president of the Sillegny Seventh Armored Division Association. He spoke no English, but we were able to communicate with each other with the help of Jean-Marc Grunfelder and an English teacher that Jean-Marc asked to join our group. Jean-Marc Tabard was able to fill in some of the missing pieces of what happened in September of 1944.

Jean-Marc Grunfelder insisted on buying our lunch at the festival. We had omelets and hamburger steaks with French fries on top, bread, and drinks and ice cream for dessert. A couple who sat at the table with us brought a special bottle of wine to share. It was a fantastic lunch with new friends.

After lunch, the mayor interviewed me about Dad's story. Pictures were taken, and he said the story would be in the local paper. About a week after returning to the United States, Jean-Marc sent me a photocopy of the article.

Melody and I spent an incredible two hours with the people of Sillegny. Our friend Bonnie Rupe said, "There are no coincidences. Things happen for a reason." As luck would have it, the day we were in Sillegny was a holiday, people were off work, there was a town festival, and everyone was in town. Also, it was a beautiful day—there are no coincidences. It was meant to be.

I want to say thank you to Jean-Marc Grunfelder and his wife for their caring and their friendship. When it was time to leave, we all exchanged home addresses and e-mail addresses, shook hands, and hugged. The last thing Jean-Marc said was "Thank you for your dad's sacrifice for my country." Needless to say, Melody and I were very emotional. There was not a dry eye.

Jean-Marc, I would like to say to you, "Thank you for remembering."

APPENDIX 1

Monuments and Memorials

T OWNS THE AUTHOR AND his wife toured in France that had monuments or memorials to the Third Army, XX Corps, or the Seventh Armored Division.

1. Avranches—Patton Square. Memorial to the "Liberator of Avranches." On display is a tank, an obelisk with the major engagements of the Third Army listed, and a Patton statue.

2. Courville-sur-Eure—A plaque on a bridge in memory of James Gomer of the Seventh Armored Division.

3. Chartres—A plaque in the garden at Station 6 of the Chemin de Memoire (Road of Memory) near the Chartres Cathedral at the Esplanade de Resistance adjacent to the Place du Chatelet.

4. Melun—A road named after the Seventh Armored Division. "Avenue de la 7eme Division Blindee Americaine." Near the south bridge.

5. Nangis—A plaque on a stone monument honoring the liberation of Nangis by the Seventh Armored Division. At the corner of Ave. de Verdun (D149) and Rue des Aubepines near the Carrefour Market.

6. Verdun—A road dedicated to the liberation of Verdun. "Rue de la 7eme Division Blindee USA."

7. Sillegny—A stone monument displaying the Seventh Armored Division shoulder patch. In memory of the Americans who fought and died at Sillegny. Corner of En Chenirue (D67) and Imp de Mauvezin.

APPENDIX 2

Selected Readings

1. *The Lorraine Campaign: U.S. Army in World War II: European Theater of Operations* by Hugh M. Cole
2. *Three Battles: Arnaville, Altuzzo, and Schmidt* by United States Army
3. *Patton at Bay: The Lorraine Campaign, 1944* by John Nelson Rickard
4. *Patton & His Third Army* by Brenton G. Wallace
5. *Gray Ghost: R.M.S. Queen Mary at War* by Stephen Harding
6. *Patton's Third Army in World War II* by Michael Green and James D. Brown
7. *Lorraine 1944—Patton vs. Manteuffel* by Steven J. Zaloga
8. *The Comet Connection: Escape from Hitler's Europe* by George Watt
9. *Northern France* by United States Army
10. *Seventh Armored Division History Books*, volumes 1 and 2 by Seventh Armored Division Association
11. *Time Life History of World War II* by Time Life Books
12. *Red Ball Express: Supply Line from the D-Day Beaches* by Pat Ware.
13. *POL on the Red Ball Express* by Dr. Steven E. Anders
14. *Operation Cobra: Combat Studies Institute, Battlebook 21* by United States Army
15. *Reduction of Fortress Metz—1 Sept. to 6 Dec. 1944* by United States Army
16. *Ghost Corps thru Hell and High Water* by XX Corps, United States Army

17. *After Action Report: Third US Army, 1 Aug. 44-9 May '45* by United States Army

18. *After Action Report: Thirty-eighth Armored Infantry Battalion, Sept. 44-Mar. 1945* by United States Army

19. *After Action Report, Seventh Armored Division, Aug.-Sep '44* by United States Army

20. *After Action Report, CCA, Aug. '44 to Aug. '45* by United States Army

21. *After Action Report, CCB, Aug. '44 to Aug. '45* by United States Army

22. *After Action Report, CCR, Aug. '44 to Aug. '45* by United States Army

23. *Morning Report, Thirty-Eighth Armored Infantry Battalion* by United States Army

24. *XX Corps Operational Reports* by United States Army

25. Seventh Armored Division Association at http://www.7tharmddiv.org

26. The *Queen Mary* Museum, Long Beach, California, at http://www.queenmary.com/our-story/Our-Story.php

27. Patton Museum, Fort Knox, Kentucky, at http://www.generalpatton.org

28. Sillegny, Municipalite, Bulletin Municipal, juillet 2009 at http://www.sillegny.fr/accueil

28. *Patton's Third Army* by Charles Province

30. Australian War Memorial at http://www.awm.gov.au/search/collections/?q=queen+mary

31. *Queen Mary* Record of Wartime Cruises at http://ww2troopships.com/ships/q/queenmary

APPENDIX 3

Picture and Image Credits

Fig. 1. Hubley map

Fig. 2. Hubley photo

Fig. 3. Hubley photo

Fig. 4. Hubley photo

Fig. 5. US Army

Fig. 6. US Navy photo

Fig. 7. J. Kent Layton Collection

Fig. 8. Hubley map

Fig. 9. Hubley photo

Fig. 10. Hubley photo

Fig. 11. Cole Land Transportation

Fig. 12. Hubley map

Fig. 13. Hubley photo

Fig. 14. Hubley photo

Fig. 15. Hubley photo

Fig. 16. Hubley map

Fig. 17. Three Battles: Arnaville, Altuzzo, and Schmidt

Fig. 18. The Lorraine Campaign

Fig. 19. Base map Google

Fig. 20. Hubley photo

Fig. 21. The Lorraine Campaign

Fig. 22. The Lorraine Campaign

Fig. 23. Cincinnati Reds

Fig. 24. Hubley photo Museum

Fig. 25. Hubley photo

Fig. 26. Hubley photo

Base maps for Fig. 1, Fig. 8, Fig. 12, and Fig. 16 are from the US State Department.

NOTES

1. Hugh M. Cole, *The Lorraine Campaign: U.S. Army in World War II: European Theater of Operations* (Washington, DC: Center for Military History, 1950), 5.

2. Ibid., 5.

3. Ibid., 5.

4. "Camp Fannin," *Wikipedia*, The Free Encyclopedia, accessed March 2013, http://en.wikipedia.org/wiki/Camp_Fannin.

5. "Fort Benning," *Wikipedia*, The Free Encyclopedia, accessed March 2013, http://en.wikipedia.org/wiki/Fort_Benning.

6. "Camp Miles Standish," *Wikipedia*, The Free Encyclopedia, accessed March 2013, http://en.wikipedia.org/wiki/Camp_Miles_Standish.

7. "Camp Shanks," *Wikipedia*, The Free Encyclopedia, accessed March 2013, http://en.wikipedia.org/wiki/Camp_Shanks.

8. Stephen Harding, *Gray Ghost: The R.M.S. Queen Mary at War* (Missoula, MT: Pictorial Histories Publishing Company, 1982).

9. "RMS *Queen Mary*," *Wikipedia*, The Free Encyclopedia, accessed March 2013, http://en.wikipedia.org/wiki/RMS_Queen_Mary.

10. "Our Story," The *Queen Mary* Museum, accessed January 2013, http://www.queenmary.com/our-story/Our-Story.php.

11. Seventh Armored Division Association History Book, volume 1, *From the Beaches to the Baltic* (Scituate, MA: Digital Scanning Inc., 1982), 38.

12. Wesley Johnston, ed., *Thirty-Eighth Armored Infantry Battalion Morning Report*, Seventh Armored Division Association, http://www.Seventharmddiv.org/docrep/ 2013.

13. "Half-track," *Wikipedia*, The Free Encyclopedia, accessed March 2013, http://en.wikipedia.org/wiki/Half-track.

14. *From the Beaches to the Baltic*, 39.

15. *Northern France*, The US Army Campaigns of World War II, Military Brochure (Washington, DC: Center of Military History, 1950), 22.

16. Walton H. Walker, *The Campaigns of Normandy and France—XX Corps Operational Report 1 Aug.-1 Sept. 1944* (Carlisle, MD: Military History Institute), part 5.

17. Ibid., part 6.

18. Cole, *The Lorraine Campaign*, 5.

19. Joseph Driscoll, *Drive of the Ghost Corps: Ghost Corps thru Hell and High Water* (Fort Leavenworth, KS: Combined Arms Research Library), 9.

20. George S. Patton, *Commendation: Ghost Corps thru Hell and High Water* (Fort Leavenworth, KS: Combined Arms Research Library), 6.

21. *Ghost Corps thru Hell and High Water* (Fort Leavenworth, KS: Combined Arms Research Library), 7.

22. Steven E. Anders, *POL on the Red Ball Express* (Quartermaster Professional Bulletin, Spring 1989).

23. *From the Beaches to the Baltic*, 43.

24. *After Action Report: Thirty-Eighth Armored Infantry Battalion— Sep '44* (Fort Leavenworth, KS: Combined Arms Research library).

25. Cole, *The Lorraine Campaign,* 173.

26. Johnston, ed., *Thirty-Eighth Armored Infantry Battalion Morning Report.*

27. Cole, *The Lorraine Campaign*, 29.

28. Ibid., 123.

29. Ibid., 142.

30. Ibid., 135-146.

31. Ibid., 171.

32. Ibid., 172.

33. *After Action Report Thirty-Eighth Armored Infantry Battalion—* Sep '44.

34. Cole, *The Lorraine Campaign,* 593.

35. Ibid., 592.

36. Harding, *Gray Ghost: The R.M.S. Queen Mary at War.*

37. George S. Patton, *Soldiers of the Third Army, Past and Present APO 403 General Orders Number 98* (Fort Knox, KY: US Army 1945).

BIBLIOGRAPHY

After Action Report Thirty-Eighth Armored Infantry Battalion—Sep '44. Fort Leavenworth, KS: Combined Arms Research Library. 1945.

Anders, Steven E. *POL on the Red Ball Express.* Fort Lee, VA: Quartermaster Professional Bulletin, 1989.

Cole, Hugh M. *The Lorraine Campaign.* US Army in World War II: European Theater of Operations. Washington, DC: Center for Military History, 1950.

Driscoll, Joseph. *Drive of the Ghost Corps.* Ghost Corps thru Hell and High Water. Fort Leavenworth, KS: Combined Arms Research Library.

Ghost Corps thru Hell and High Water. Fort Leavenworth, KS: Combined Arms Research Library.

Harding, Stephen. *Gray Ghost: The R.M.S. Queen Mary at War.* Missoula, MT: Pictorial Histories Publishing Company, 1982.

Hubley, Rankin Dale. Personal diary. 1991.

Johnston, Wesley. ed. "Battalion-Level Officers of the Thirty-Eighth Armored Infantry Battalion." Seventh Armored Division Association. Accessed 2009. http://www.Seventharmddiv.org/38aib.htm.

Johnston, Wesley. ed. "Thirty-Eighth Armored Infantry Battalion Morning Report." Seventh Armored Division Association, http://www.Seventharmddiv.org/docrep/ 2013.

Northern France. *The US Army Campaigns of World War II.* Washington DC: Center of Military History, 1950.

Patton, George S. *Soldiers of the Third Army, Past and Present.* APO 403 General Orders 98. Fort Knox, KY: Patton Museum, 1945.

The *Queen Mary* Museum. "Our Story." Long Beach, California. http://www.queenmary.com/our-story/war-stats.php.

Seventh Armored Division Association History Book, volume 1. *From the Beaches to the Baltic.* Scituate, MA: Digital Scanning Inc., 1982.

Walker, Walton H. *The Campaigns of Normandy and France—XX Corps Operational Report 1 Aug.-1 Sept. 1944.* Carlisle, MD: Military History Institute, 1944.

Wikipedia, The Free Encyclopedia. Wikimedia Foundation Inc.